Published by Ice House Books

Copyright © 2019 Ice House Books

Written by Moira Butterfield
Illustrated by Pedro Demetriou
Designed by Emily Curtis

Ice House Books is an imprint of Half Moon Bay Limited
The Ice House, 124 Walcot Street, Bath, BA1 5BG
www.icehousebooks.co.uk

ISBN 978-1-912867-12-7

Printed in China

WHEN ALL YOUR FRIENDS ARE ALIENS...

ICE HOUSE BOOKS

WHEN YOU THINK A SPACESHIP IS IN YOUR NEIGHBOURHOOD

HAS SOMETHING WEIRD BUZZED INTO THE SKY NEAR YOU?

Before you panic about a space-alien invasion, back up a minute. How can you tell it's a UFO from space and not a drone or a kid's flying toy? Work through this **HANDY CHECKLIST**.

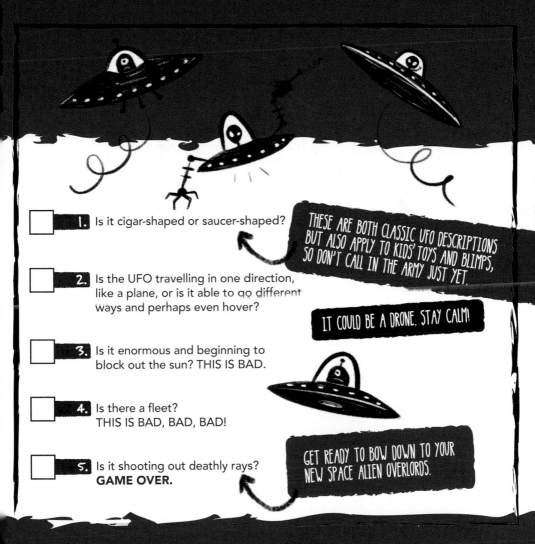

1. Is it cigar-shaped or saucer-shaped?

THESE ARE BOTH CLASSIC UFO DESCRIPTIONS BUT ALSO APPLY TO KIDS' TOYS AND BLIMPS, SO DON'T CALL IN THE ARMY JUST YET.

2. Is the UFO travelling in one direction, like a plane, or is it able to go different ways and perhaps even hover?

IT COULD BE A DRONE. STAY CALM!

3. Is it enormous and beginning to block out the sun? THIS IS BAD.

4. Is there a fleet? THIS IS BAD, BAD, BAD!

GET READY TO BOW DOWN TO YOUR NEW SPACE ALIEN OVERLORDS.

5. Is it shooting out deathly rays? **GAME OVER.**

WHEN YOU NEED TO KNOW YOUR SPACE ALIENS

WHICH SPACE ALIENS ARE YOU DEALING WITH? HERE ARE SOME GENERAL TYPES WHO APPEAR IN SCI-FI MOVIES AND BOOKS.

1. ROBOT

An old-school space-alien machine beloved of 1950s movies. The classic way to defeat it is to confuse it so it blows its circuits. Ask it to explain the plot of *The Matrix* or who's who in *Game of Thrones*.

2. MANY-ARMED BLOBBY
Think gross, possibly even dripping. A body shape like play slime.

3. HUMANOID
A shape-shifter disguised as a human until push comes to shove and it turns into space alien number 3. It may get careless and accidentally give itself away by going slightly green or flicking out a lizard tongue.

4. ROSWELL LOCAL
A stick-thin body with a heart-shaped face and eyes like a cat. These space aliens are said to regularly visit Roswell in New Mexico, and their hobby is abducting humans. It's not clear whether they are experimenting on people or just having a laugh.

WHEN YOU WANT TO COMMUNICATE WITH A SPACE ALIEN

ASSUMING YOU MEET A FRIENDLY SPACE ALIEN, HOW SHOULD YOU TRY TO COMMUNICATE?

DO SAY:

WELCOME!

Use unthreatening sign language, perhaps holding your hands up to show you are unarmed, and then beckoning them to follow you to a handy community leader.

DON'T SAY:

WHEN SPACE ALIENS TAKE YOU ON A TRIP

HOW SHOULD YOU BEHAVE IF SPACE ALIENS ABDUCT YOU?

Don't forget you are representing humankind, so try not to be embarrassing. Don't panic so much you leave a shameful puddle. The world needs you to be **IMPRESSIVE**, not incontinent.

The sooner you co-operate, the sooner you can get back home to tell your incredible story and **BREAK THE INTERNET.**

Remember to post a **SELFIE**. #spacealieninvasionlolz

Think of it as like going to the dentist for an **INTERGALACTIC CHECK-UP.** A few minutes of poking around and a rinse, you're outta there.

WHEN SPACE ALIENS TAKE YOU ON A TRIP

WHAT SHOULD YOU DO WHEN YOU GET HOME FROM A SPACE-ALIEN ABDUCTION? HERE IS SOME ENCOUNTER ADVICE.

FIRST: Use soothing cream on any sore parts.

THEN: Appear on TV, but be warned that you may be put on shows that specialise in crazy people who think they are cats or Napoleon.

THEN: Do your own podcast, re-enacting your trip with a friend wrapped in foil and some kitchen bits and pieces such as a turkey baster and funnel doubling up as space-alien medical equipment.

THEN: Write up a movie script with you as the hero, persuading the space aliens to leave: "Earth is really watery, like a dirty hot tub. Go to Mars instead. It smells of chocolate."

WHEN THERE'S A FULL-ON SPACE ALIEN INVASION

HERE ARE FOUR SUGGESTIONS FOR REACTING TO A SPACE-ALIEN TAKEOVER OF EARTH.

SNEEZE ON THEM
They may have no defence against human germs.

ACHOO!

ALL-OUT FIGHT
Use all the weapons on Earth and steal the space aliens' weapons, too. Use their own super-powered stuff against them and see how they like it.

OUTSMART THEM
Find their weakness. It could be something we have on Earth but they have never tried, such as peanut butter or bubble bath. Anything's worth a try.

ASSIMILATE
Mix with the space aliens and perhaps even have space-alien/human children. They could turn out to be super-bright humans or super-dumb space aliens. You'll love them anyway, tentacles and all.

WHEN THERE'S A FULL-ON SPACE ALIEN INVASION

HERE ARE FOUR THINGS YOU SHOULD <u>NOT</u> DO IF SPACE ALIENS TAKE OVER EARTH.

DON'T underestimate them. They may have skills you don't possess, such as super-smell or the ability to see around corners. In sci-fi shows the heroes usually find these out quickly by 'accidentally' sacrificing an expendable character. Do you have a friend you won't miss?

DON'T ignore them. They may have stopped off to eat you, like a quick snack at a space service station. You may need to hide.

DON'T launch all of Earth's weapons at once and then find out the space aliens have a kick-ass missile shield. That would be Earth-shakingly dumb.

DON'T assume the space aliens you meet are just like you. Their brains could literally be in their butts, for example. **PROCEED CAUTIOUSLY.**

WHEN SPACE ALIENS HAVE BECOME YOUR OVERLORDS

YOU'LL NEED WAYS TO SURVIVE IF SPACE ALIENS HAVE TAKEN CHARGE.

Do they show a worrying taste for **HUMAN DINNER**? Get them interested in sausages and meat-feast pizzas instead.

IF THEY HAVE DESTROYED YOUR NEIGHBOURHOOD go to live somewhere out in the wilds, off the grid, where you can be free. But be warned – there will be no internet. Your computer technology is likely to be as useful as a chocolate teapot from now on.

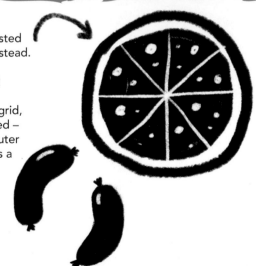

Make yourself a **TRUSTED SPACE ALIEN ADVISOR.** Learn their language, customs and beliefs, so they let you into their inner circle … and **THEN ZAP THOSE OVER-TRUSTING INTERGALACTIC IDIOTS!**

Give up and become a **SPACE ALIEN'S SLAVE.** Enjoy the lack of responsibility and the set drool-wiping, tentacle-massaging routine as best you can.

WHEN A SPACE ALIEN GETS CRANKY

SPOT THE SIGNS THAT YOUR SPACE ALIEN FRIEND MIGHT BE ABOUT TO LOSE CONTROL AND GET SUPER-NOVA ANGRY.

- It changes colour, like an octopus does when it's crabby.

- It begins to make a weird noise, such as hissing or growling. This is bad in snakes and tigers, but super-bad in space dudes.

- It gets out a ray gun. Stay very still, so you don't become a target. You could trip up somebody nearby to draw the fire.

- It loses its cool completely, starts grabbing nearby life forms and gobbles them up. Give it some space for a while.

WHEN YOU GET INTO A FIGHT WITH A SPACE ALIEN

HERE ARE SOME ANTI-SPACE-ALIEN MOVES. GOOD LUCK.

METAL ROBOT SPACE ALIEN
Confuse it to make it blow itself up. Give it a computer virus to make it crash or pull the plug out when it's charging.

HUMANOID
Make it have human feelings so it feels love (the classic *Star Trek* move). Then, while it's crying, blow it to smithereens with a tank.

MANY-ARMED BLOBBY
Chop off bits with a garden spade
until it gets fed up and slithers away.

ROSWELL LOCAL
There are rumours that dead space aliens have been
found in space wreckage and stored at a secret US
Army base at Roswell. You could remind your alien
of this: "I know where your granny is, triangle head.
Wanna try something?"

Show any unwanted alien a sci-fi movie and say: "Watch and
learn, my friend" – the space aliens always lose in the end.

WHEN YOU WANT TO SPOT A SECRET SPACE ALIEN

SOME PEOPLE THINK THAT SPACE ALIENS ARE ALREADY HIDING AMONGST US. WHAT ARE THE SIGNS?

SPACE ALIEN?
Do you know someone with a lizard-like appearance – perhaps a slightly scaly skin? They could be a reptile-alien, or just your grandma. You decide.

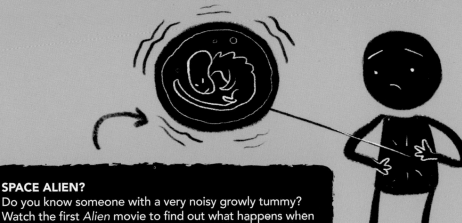

SPACE ALIEN?
Do you know someone with a very noisy growly tummy? Watch the first *Alien* movie to find out what happens when something from outer space finds a nice warm stomach…

SPACE ALIEN?
Do you know someone who wears really stupid mirror-reflective sunglasses all the time? Perhaps they're just a dork, but they could be trying to hide eyes that glow like car lights.

SPACE ALIEN?
Do you know someone who always orders the greenest, most outlandish cocktail going, and likes to hang out with a weird crowd? Watch the famous space-alien Cantina bar scene in *Star Wars*. Can you spot them?

WHEN YOU WANT TO SPOT A CELEBRITY SPACE ALIEN

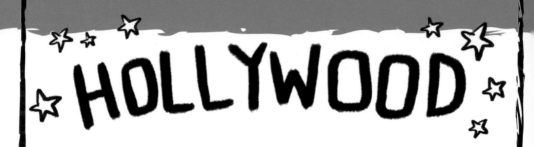

HOLLYWOOD

SOME SAY THAT SPACE ALIENS ARE HANGING OUT AMONGST US IN PLAIN SIGHT, AS CELEBRITIES AND WORLD LEADERS. HOW CAN WE TELL?

Some celebs wear sunglasses indoors.
IS THIS BECAUSE THEY HAVE NO EYE PUPILS?

When celebs look as if they've had plastic surgery.
IS IT REALLY THEIR HUMAN DISGUISE SLOWLY MELTING?

Some celebs say crazy things on social media.
HAVE THEY FORGOTTEN THEY NEED TO MAKE SENSE TO HUMANS?

Some celebs seem to be famous for no reason.
ARE THEIR TALENTS ONLY VISIBLE IN ANOTHER TIME-SPACE DIMENSION?

Some world leaders seem insane.
ARE THEY JUST INTERGALACTICALLY CHALLENGED?

WHEN ALL YOUR FRIENDS ARE SPACE ALIENS

WELL DONE IF YOU HAVE LOTS OF SPACE ALIEN FRIENDS. YOU ARE A TRULY UNIVERSAL PERSON. HERE ARE SOME TIPS FOR GETTING ALONG WITH THEM.

DO get them talking by asking them about their home in space, though be careful to avoid space bores who like to boast about their endless trips to fashionable nebulae.

DO assure them that your home is a ray-gun-free zone.

DO tactfully draw attention to any space-alien body parts that have accidentally slipped out, such as tails or tentacles. Your friends will no doubt be trying their best to fit in, but may have occasional wardrobe failures.

DO throw parties. Aliens love parties. You could have a dress code of asteroid belts and moon boots, and serve ice-cream sundaes with melted Mars Bars and space dust. Both of these are great glories of our planet.

PARTY LIKE A SUPERNOVA!

WHEN ALL YOUR FRIENDS ARE SPACE ALIENS

IT'S ALL TOO EASY TO MAKE A HUMAN-CENTRIC GAFFE WITH ALIEN FRIENDS. TRY TO BE TACTFUL AND ALIEN-AWARE.

DON'T mention the many movies in which they and their friends are negatively portrayed. It's space-ist.

DON'T assume that they're all as clever as a *Star Trek* Vulcan. Some of them might be as thick as space rock.

DON'T put a saucepan on your head and do your terrible impression of Darth Vader.

DON'T suggest a game of Space Invaders or Halo. Things could get awkward when you obliterate the space aliens onscreen, while whooping loudly.

DON'T stare or make comments such as: "Let me give you a hand, or seven!". Your friend could be hyper-sensitive about extra body parts.

WHEN YOU NEED TO TELL THE GENDER OF A SPACE ALIEN

Just like the creatures on our own planet, aliens have all sorts of gender variations. They may have both male and female body parts, like snails, or they might naturally change genders during their lifetime, like some fishes. The best way to approach the question might be to **COME RIGHT OUT AND ASK**, perhaps after a few intergalactic cocktails.

Don't assume that **SPACE ALIEN BABIES** will be like humans. Space tots might hatch from eggs in a nest or your alien friends might simply divide themselves in two, like an amoeba. If your friend is expecting, be prepared to lay extra places at dinner at short notice, and you may need to knit more baby booties than you think.

WHEN YOU WANT TO DATE A SPACE ALIEN

DO YOU FANCY AN ALIEN AND WANT TO ASK THEM OUT?
TRY ONE OF THESE STARRY CHAT-UP LINES.

You have such an inner glow.
Is it kryptonite?

Are your folks from Venus?
Cos you're out of this world.*

*Officially the cheesiest chat-up line in the known universe.

WHEN YOU MOVE IN WITH A SPACE ALIEN

SO YOU WANT TO TAKE A BIG STEP FOR MANKIND AND MOVE IN WITH A SPACE ALIEN PARTNER. THERE ARE PROS AND CONS:

PRO Your space alien partner may have a superfast way of doing the housework, such as multi-armed dusting. **CON** Your space alien partner may turn out to be a despotic all-powerful overlord, in which case you'll be taking out the trash every time.

PRO You may get the opportunity to visit your partner's home planet.
CON Your in-laws may be less human-friendly than your partner. If they invite you to dinner, check that you're not on the menu. If you invite them to visit you on Earth, be clear they can't bring a whole fleet.

PRO Your partner may glow in the dark, which will save on energy bills.
CON Your partner may have a secret abducting habit, which could irritate the neighbours.

WARNING: RISK OF HEARTBREAK
There's always the chance that you might just be a temporary experiment and your partner might one day leave for another galaxy, leaving you staring at the stars with a broken heart.
If this happens, go to Roswell and wait for another space date to come along and pick you up.

WHEN YOU WANT TO MAKE SPACE ALIENS LAUGH

WHEN FACED WITH A RAY GUN, TRY A JOKE TO LIGHTEN THE MOOD. SPACE ALIENS CAN BE A TOUGH AUDIENCE, THOUGH, AND WITH THESE JOKES YOUR PERFORMANCE MAY BE OVER AT WARP SPEED.

Why are space aliens messy drinkers? WITH FLYING SAUCERS, IT'S HARD NOT TO SPILL.

How do you get a baby space alien to sleep? ROCKET.

Why don't space aliens celebrate Christmas?
They don't like to give away THEIR PRESENCE.

What's E.T. short for?
BECAUSE HE'S GOT LITTLE LEGS.

What do you call an unhealthy alien?
AN EXTRA CHOLESTEROL.

Why did the space aliens
leave the bar on the Moon?
IT HAD NO ATMOSPHERE.

WHEN YOU WANT TO BUY A PRESENT FOR A SPACE ALIEN

WHY NOT BUY YOUR ALIEN PAL A PRESENT TO SHOW YOU APPRECIATE THEIR VISIT? HERE ARE SOME SPACE-TASTIC SUGGESTIONS:

- A new **WARP DRIVE UNIVERSE RESONATOR** for their spaceship. Or a screwdriver.

- **A PROBING WEEKEND** in Roswell.

- A box of **MOONCAKES.**

JUST VISITING

ALIEN ONBOARD

MAKE MARS GREAT AGAIN

WHEN SPACE ALIENS COME TO DINNER

IF YOU ARE COOKING A MEAL FOR SPACE VISITORS, MAKE SURE YOU PLAN-ET!

If your guest alien looks like a prawn, **DON'T SERVE PRAWNS.** You're asking for a ray gun zap right there.

If your guest is a many-toothed monster who tears lumps out of his enemies, go with **BURGERS.**

Alien robots may eat electricity, so offer them a delicious **PLUG AND LEAD.**

Be clear that humans aren't on the menu by offering only vegetarian options. But don't serve tofu. **VERY FEW BEINGS IN THE UNIVERSE CAN STOMACH IT.**

DO NOT offer your friend **JELLYBABIES.** They may get very confused.

WHEN YOUR BOSS IS A SPACE ALIEN

HOW SHOULD YOU HANDLE AN EXTRA-TERRESTRIAL OVERLORD IN THE OFFICE?

- Watch out if your boss suddenly super-sizes and grows tentacles. It could be a **BAD MOOD DAY.**

- **DON'T IGNORE THEIR ORDERS** unless you have an escape plan and a ray gun stashed in your desk.

- Be on your guard if they use the word **PROBE** instead of appraisal.

- Don't suck up to your boss. They may suck back and **NOBODY WANTS TO SEE THAT MESS.**

- If your boss gives you a rocket, expect to be **FIRED.**

WHEN YOUR PET IS A SPACE ALIEN

SMALL ALIENS CAN MAKE DELIGHTFUL PETS.
MANY PEOPLE ALREADY HAVE THEM WITHOUT REALISING.

Most **DOMESTIC CATS** are space aliens. Where else would they be disappearing off to every day but to see their fellow kind?

PUGS AND DACHSHUNDS are definitely space aliens. Come on. Just look at them!

HAMSTERS are thought to come from Alpha Centauri, and when they squeak they are actually saying: "Kill the humans!"

TORTOISES were designed as Martian attack robots with the ability to travel at light speed and do immense calculations. Unfortunately they need charging and their inventor forgot to add a USB port.

WHEN A SPACE ALIEN IS TRYING TO TAKE OVER YOUR MIND

SPACE ALIENS HAVE A BAD HABIT FOR CONTROLLING MINDS. ARE YOU SUSPICIOUS THAT ONE OF THOSE EXTRA-T BAD BOYS IS BEGINNING TO TAKE YOU OVER? WATCH OUT FOR THESE FIVE SERIOUS TELL-TALE SIGNS.

1. You keep having the same dream – that you are Lord High Emperor of Earth and you have a hover-throne.

2. Your head seems to be changing shape and getting more pointy.

3. You don't feel yourself. You feel half-borg.

4. You beep every ten minutes.

5. For some reason you have decided to move to Roswell.

WHEN YOU NEED TO FAKE BEING A SPACE ALIEN

IF THE WHOLE WORLD GETS TAKEN OVER BY SPACE ALIENS YOU COULD BE THE LAST HUMAN LEFT. YOU MAY NEED TO START FAKING IT TO FIT IN.

POST A SELFIE wearing green face make-up. Use chopsticks and tennis balls to make antennae.

FAKE A SPACESHIP PHOTO by throwing a hubcap, then show it round and boast about your latest vehicle.

Wear **GLOW-IN-THE-DARK CLOTHING** and only go out at night.

When other aliens ask you if you've seen any humans, say: **"NO. SORRY. I ATE THE LAST ONE."**

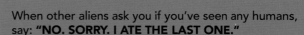

Get used to being the last human. Make the best of it and **DON'T LET US DOWN WITH BAD MANNERS!** Eating soup with the correct spoon is what makes us different from the rest of the sloppy species in the universe.

WHEN YOU WANT TO BUILD YOUR OWN ALIEN-STYLE SPACESHIP

HERE ARE SOME CLASSIC SCI-FI MOVIE SPACESHIP DESIGNS SHOULD YOU DECIDE TO ESCAPE AN ALIEN-INFESTED EARTH AND GO ON YOUR OWN JOURNEY INTO OUTER SPACE.

THE FLYING SAUCER

Likely to be very wobbly and have major aerodynamic issues, but you'll appreciate it if you are a fan of retro design.
You could furnish it with a waterbed and some lava lamps.

MASSIVE MEGA-SHIP

The Darth Vader option. This is a little 'showy-offy', and may get a negative reaction: "Whoever drives that has got to be from Uranus."

CLOAKING DEVICE

To make your spaceship invisible to enemies, and great for illegal parking.

TWO-ALIEN POD

A small easy-to-manage tin-can shape, which is nippy for hurtling through asteroid clouds. This design tends to be piloted by mavericks in sci-fi movies, so it has a certain cool rebel style, but it may get claustrophobic and smelly on long journeys. (Never open the window, though.)

WHEN YOU WANT TO BUILD YOUR OWN ALIEN-STYLE SPACESHIP

HERE ARE SOME DESIGN IDEAS FOR SPACESHIP INTERIORS, SCI-FI MOVIE STYLE.

INDUSTRIAL
Bits of clanging metal hanging down, pipes and gantries, as if below decks in a container ship. Think *Alien*. A menacing vibe and a lack of carpets.

CORPORATE

Loads of levels and corridors patrolled by armed soldiers. Think *Star Wars*. Lacks the human touch (there is no room for wall posters or pot plants in the Empire).

NEW AGE

This interior style mainly appears in early episodes of *Star Trek*, whenever peaceful super-beings come along to impart mystical truths. Their ships have bead curtains, cushions and music. Yeah, man. We are all stardust, ok?

FLAT PACK

The classic human-built space-station mode – modules connected together and filled with equipment such as experiments and spacesuits. Astronauts float around inside along with crumbs, dropped toothbrushes and socks. A bit 'slackers in space'.

WHEN SOMEONE SAYS THAT YOU'RE A SPACE ALIEN

WHAT SHOULD YOU DO IF SOMEONE ACCUSES YOU OF BEING AN EXTRA-TERRESTRIAL ENTITY?

- Dial down on the blue hair and the purple contact lenses. You could be overdoing the 'possible alien' look.

- Are you being mistaken for E.T.? Try a new skin cream, perhaps?

- Make sure you never probe in public.

WHEN YOU'RE A SPACE ALIEN AND YOU WANT TO HIDE IT

Become an author and write a book about space aliens,
FULL OF STUFF THAT SOUNDS TOTALLY MADE UP.
Nobody will suspect you …